HEARING

Wayne Jackman

Reading consultant:
Diana Bentley
University of Reading

Photographs by
Chris Fairclough

The Senses

Touch
Sight
Hearing
Smell
Taste

Editor: Janet De Saulles

First published in 1989 by
Wayland (Publishers) Ltd
61 Western Road, Hove
East Sussex, BN3 1JD, England

British Library Cataloguing in Publication Data
Jackman, Wayne
  Hearing.
  1. Man. Hearing. For children
  I. Title   II. Fairclough, Chris   III. Series
  612'.85

  ISBN 1–85210–734–0

Phototypeset by Kalligraphics Ltd, Horley, Surrey, England
Printed and bound by Casterman S.A., Belgium

Contents

All the words that appear
in **bold** are explained in the
glossary on page 22.

We hear with our ears.

There are five **senses** – sight, touch, smell, hearing and taste. This book is about hearing. We use our ears to hear things. The children in the picture opposite can hear their teacher call to them. The boy in the picture below is standing on the pavement, well away from the traffic. It is too loud for him. What noises can you hear?

Nice or nasty sounds.

Some sounds are very enjoyable. Music can make us happy. Other sounds can be unpleasant. Has a roadworker ever drilled in the road near your house? I bet it drove you mad. Some sounds warn us of danger. The policeman in the picture opposite has put on his **siren** to tell everyone that he is in a hurry.

Loud or quiet sounds.

Some sounds are very quiet and we need help to hear them. Maybe a doctor has listened to your chest with a **stethoscope**? This makes the noise inside sound louder. The doctor can then find out if you are ill. There are other noises we can hear very clearly – even when we do not want to. Perhaps you have a baby sister or brother who wakes you up at night!

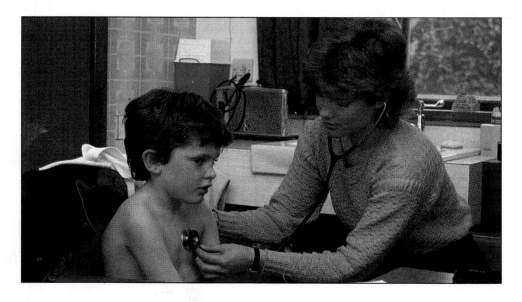

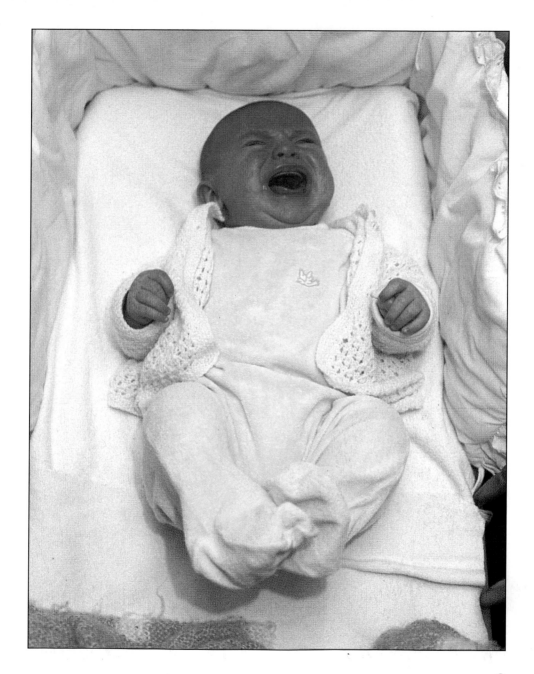

How do I hear?

Have you ever thrown a stone into a pond? When the stone touches the water it makes ripples. Although we cannot see sound the way we can see the ripples in the water, this is rather like what happens when something makes a noise. Each sound makes **invisible** waves in the air which travel until they reach our ears. Our ears send the messages to our **brains** and we can understand what the noise means.

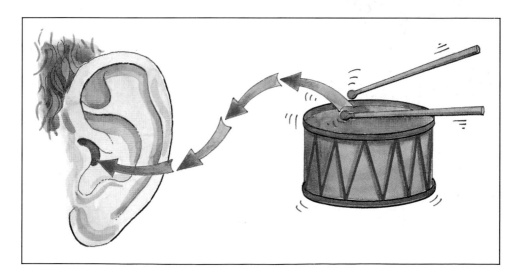

A balloon trick.

Although we cannot see the sound waves themselves, we can see how they work. Blow up a balloon and knot it. Ask a friend to hold the balloon between his or her hands. Now take a cardboard tube and rest it on the balloon. Talk down the tube. The sound waves from your voice will make the balloon **vibrate**.

Pardon? I cannot hear you.

Some people cannot hear. They are deaf. Imagine what that must be like. How would you hear the telephone or the door-bell? Some deaf people can understand words by looking at our mouths. This is called **lip-reading**. Deaf people often talk to each other using their hands to make signs.

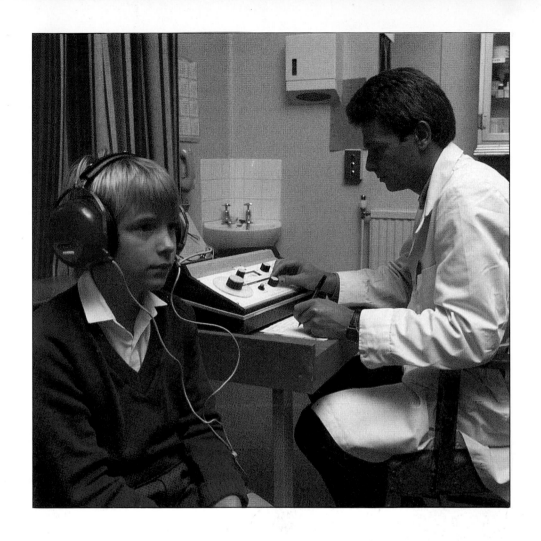

Some people are not completely deaf. They use a hearing aid which makes things sound louder. The child in the above photo is having his hearing tested.

What a strange shape!

A lot of animals have big, upright ears. They can move their ears in many directions to catch sounds and to listen out for their enemies. Have you ever seen a cat do this? Humans do not have many enemies so our ears are smaller and less sensitive than animals' ears. They are, however, very good for hearing many sounds coming from different directions at the same time.

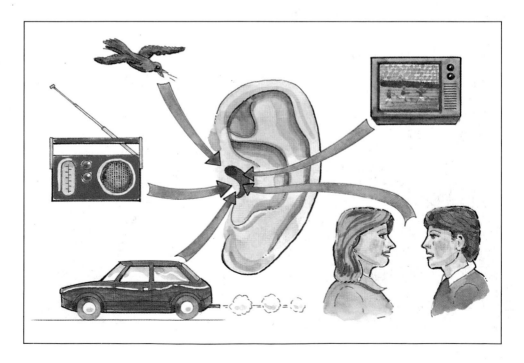

How we learn to talk.

Without our sense of hearing we would never learn to talk. Babies hear sounds made by parents and older children. They start to copy them as a way of trying them out. Eventually they put sounds together to make speech. If no one ever spoke to a baby, it would never hear sounds to copy. Then it would not learn to speak a language.

Games for you and your friends.

1. Get into a group. Close your eyes and listen to how many different noises you can hear. Each time you notice one open your eyes and write it down. After a couple of minutes see who has heard the most sounds.

2. Blindfold a friend. Ask him or her to cover
up one ear and spin the person round. Turn
on a radio or a cassette player and move it
around. Can the blindfolded person point
towards the radio?

Glossary

Brains   Our brains control and organize the way we act, think and speak.

Invisible   Something is invisible when we cannot see it but we know that it is there.

Lip-reading   When we speak we move our lips. Some deaf people can look at the shapes our lips make and understand what words we are saying.

Senses   We use our senses to know what things look, feel, smell, sound and taste like.

Siren A type of horn which makes a loud wailing sound.

Stethoscope   This is an instrument that a doctor sometimes uses. The doctor examines the patient by listening through the two tubes of the stethoscope.

Vibrate   To wobble backwards and forwards very quickly.

Books to read

Body Facts by Alan Maryon-Davis
(Macdonald,1984)
Hearing by Henry Pluckrose (Franklin
Watts, 1985)
I Am Deaf by Brenda Pettenuzzo (Franklin
Watts, 1987)
I Hear With My Ears by Joan Mills
(Schofield & Son, 1986)
Sound by A. Webb (Franklin Watts, 1987)
Your Nose And Ears by Joan Iveson-Iveson
(Wayland, 1985)

Acknowledgements

The author and Publisher would like to thank the Headteacher, staff
and pupils of St Bernadette's School, Atkins Road, Clapham Park,
London, for their help in producing this book. They would also like to
thank the Wayland Picture Library for the photo on page 6 and
Trevor Hill for supplying the photograph on page 15.

Index